I Am More Than a Daydream

By Jennae Cecelia

Illustrations by Riley Moran
Instagram: @gabriellescrapart

Cover Design by Islam Farid
www.islamfarid.net

I Am More Than a Daydream

ISBN: 987-1544237190

Jennae Cecelia

For my daydreamers -
You are always more

I Am More Than a Daydream

~

Contents

I Am More Than a Daydream

~

day•dream (noun)

    1.   All you want in the future.

re•al•i•ty (noun)

    1.   All you know in the present.

How often do you daydream?
For most, it is many times a day.
We stare out the window
instead of the task in front of us.
We fantasize about where we would
much rather be,
the significant other we long for,
our ideal job,
the body we hope to see in the mirror,
a healthier mindset,
pure happiness in our lives
and the lives of others,
peace in this chaotic world.
However, how many of us daydreamers
believe these pleasant thoughts will truly
turn into our reality?
Daydreams are more than just short
bursts of happiness that only our minds
can see.
I know I am more than a daydream; and
you are, too.

With love,

Jennae

All I Am

Just like the moon,
brightness is the only
side you see of me.
Darkness lingers on the
other side,
only exposed in catastrophe.

- I am the wo(man) in the moon

Raw

I stand;
water rushes down my face,
drips off my hair
and along my back.
I turn the knob;
the water scalds.
My skin quickly changes to
a vibrant shade of red.
I can't burn off the pain;
it lives inside my head.
I can only scrub so much,
before my skin becomes raw.
This shower isn't going to fix
my problems.
But I am at least trying,
right?

The pain you feel hurts me just
as much as it hurts you.
There is nothing worse than watching
the person you love ache
and there is nothing your human
strength can heal.

- *I want to be your medicine*

I wish I could be as bold
as the people who spend
the twilight hours
with their lights on and
curtains wide open.
The people who do not fear of who
is peering in on their belongings and
personal moments exchanged.

- I prefer my do not disturb signs

I went through phases
of loving
and hurting.

I went through phases
of hating
and growing.

I went through phases
of stealing kisses
and forcing laughter.

I went through phases
of burning bridges
and then attempting the rebuild.

I went through phases
of my mind yearning
and my heart burning.

I went through phases
but those phases always
cycled back to a fresh start.

- I am the new moon

Cacti

I am a cactus;
made up of thorns,
but still managing to
grow flowers.

I Am a Forest

I am the unexpected
pit stop;
one that was only intended
to last for a brief
moment so you could
catch your breath,
and refresh
before continuing on
to your destination.
You quickly learned
I am not a well-manicured shrub
trimmed daily for perfection.
I am the whole damn forest.
With 72 foot tall trees,
and flowers out-blooming the weeds.

He was as deceiving as the
false warmth of a sunny day
from a window pane in March.

- good thing I am an ice princess

Growth

I was your tree
to nourish,
but I was neglected
sun and water.
I lacked the beauty you
desired.
You chopped me down.
Little did you expect,
I now plant
myself flowers in the spot
you left vacant.
I am growing just fine
on my own.

I am the sky.
I am the plants.
I am the moon.
I am the sun.
I am the soil.
I am the wind.
I will never end.
I will live forever;
growing more
powerful,
plentiful,
peaceful.

- no evil will put an end to me

I cannot simply be read from
front to back.
I am all the moments
between the lines
of the story you already think
you have memorized.

- I am a poem with many interpretations

Our eyes met with assurance
and ease.
I felt like he could read
the book of me.
I wasn't placed down on a
nightstand for a moments rest,
nor was I skimmed over in boredom.
He read me with desire and passion.
Wanting no cliff hanger,
no melancholy ending.
I was the book filled with
highlighter marks and
notes in the margins.
I wasn't one that
would be passed on,
or borrowed.
For he knew I was filled
with many sequels.

-I am his never-ending story

I am a woman with a mouth
of wisdom.
You better be man enough to
listen with patience,
not talk over me because you
can be louder.

- you can't silence this woman

You
can
tear down
my tiny shed
made of rotted *wood*
but I will build back
a tower made of *gold*.

- *women are architects and builders*

My thoughts are purely in the present,
not distorting reality.
My mind is aligned with my body,
just like the moon pulling the tide.
One force regulating another.

- *I am zen*

Mirror Images

I catch a glimpse of my aged
secrets in the mirror
during early mornings
before my makeup is evenly painted
on my skin,
or late at night when I have
nightmares of the places my mind
once had been.
I don't ever want to be made up
of those secrets again.

I Am More Than a Daydream

~

All I Can Be

I Am More Than a Daydream

~

The cells I used to embody
no longer live inside these walls.
I have shed away the loathing
and filtered in passion.
My body is a temple
that will never be broken down.

- *I am reborn*

Stop letting creepy men scare you with
their beady eyes staring you
down with hunger.
Glare back at them until it cuts them
through their soul.

*- we shouldn't have to walk with our keys
interlocked between our fingers*

Her
outer
beauty
sprouted from
the nourishment
of her inner confidence.

- she's alive even in a drought

Scars

You turned my gray scars
into
colorful tattoos
and my mind
into
new flowers
sprouting
from the nourished roots.

Living in the same
four bedroom
three bath
house since birth
has me itching
for more than familiar walls
and knowledge of where
the floors creek.

- pack my bags, leave the baggage

We Are Desirable

We are spray tans, fake tones,
because pale now means sickly and
orange means at least you're trying.

We are eyelash extensions,
10 coats of mascara,
because if the small hairs
attached to her eyelids
have increased in a length
that are borderline wings,
then you need those too.

We are hate toward those
who resemble
what we aren't
and where we wish to be.
Because sometimes we forget that the
thin
body we are envying wants the
CURVES
you read hate letters to in
the morning mirror.

We, she, he, her, it, his, theirs, ours,
have pieces no one else will.
We are desirable.

Happiness is a personal experience.
My happiness is not your happiness.

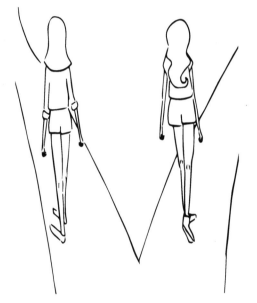

Daydream

I don't want a white picket fence life.
2.5 kids in the backyard,
my spouse and I complaining
about jobs we hate.

I want the sun and the stars.
The whole damn universe.
I want to breathe in the fresh grass
and kiss in a canoe,
on my fifth vacation of the year.

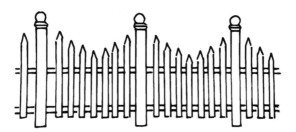

Would I still be loved if the
long hair society wants,
was chopped off into what
society hates;
women who don't all look the same?

- *eliminate gender norms*

If you saw me out now
sipping my drink with the man
who loves me madly,
I bet you would feel a
pit in your stomach and
rage in your throat.
You were the one
who thought my anxiety
was embarrassing in all
the public scenes.
With worry building
that I would ruin your
so-called image.
Now I have a hand to hold
if he sees my breathing
become uneasy.

*- how does it feel to be without
my so-called virus?*

How different would we treat
people if they were stamped
with expiration dates?
Who would we savor every
minute of, and who would we
let go to waste?

- we are all milk jugs in the end

I
wonder
if landfills
are piled with
all the changes we've made.
Love notes crumpled under broken
picture frames, surrounded by the clothes
too big from all the lost weight.
What are landfills,
other than a potluck of change?

Starving artists may be lacking
in material possessions,
but they are flourishing in
dedication to their dreams.

- I prefer happiness over diamonds

The less makeup I wear,
the more I start to connect
with the girl smiling at me
in the mirror.

- unedited is just as beautiful

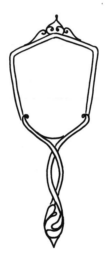

Bodies

There are many bodies on this earth.
My body of water is clear and deep,
filled with colorful fish and green plants.
Yours is shallow and murky
from the lack of weeds
being picked and toxins dripping in
that cause death to the fish.
It's time to cleanse
your body,
your mind,
your soul.

Are we working for future goals
or are we working to get by
until we are dead?
After all, the future is nothing more
than the outcome of what you are
doing in the present.

- daydreams become reality

Our moons were different
on the night of our births.
One just shy of being full,
the other barely a sliver
of a crescent.
Now I know why you made me whole.

- together we are the full moon

I have spent way too many days
staring at a dressing room mirror
saying,
*someday I'll look good in these
skinny jeans.*
But today I say,
fuck it.
I can wear what I want,
because life is too short to
care about a damn pair of pants.

- size zero or 20, you are beautiful

If you feel insecure in your relationship,
your significant other must suck and
I suggest moving on.

- love doesn't always mean security

In the end,
we have only ever seen
our faces in
reflections and pictures.
Our true beauty is
a secret to us
and maybe that's why we
are the last to believe in it.

- mirror, mirror, on the wall

You say you prefer a woman
with curves,
yet your facial expression
reads disgust
when she says she weighs 185.

Thankfully she has confidence
running over her
hips,
belly,
and thighs.
Ignoring your immature thoughts.
She can recognize an ugly mind.

- women aren't here to please your eyes

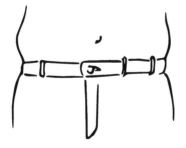

She is already a river
flooding with ideas,
and no matter how much debris,
the flow of her wisdom will never
be slowed down.

- no dam will stop her

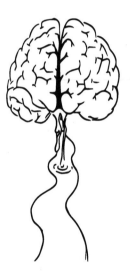

Your roots were planted eight feet
below the surface
in stale earth.
While mine were only
three inches deep,
ready to be plucked up
and planted in richer soil.

- *be adaptable*

I taught myself that
independence
does not mean
loneliness,
it means
hopefulness.

*- I found myself first before
I searched for you*

You could pluck a 1,000 flower
petals.
He loves me,
he loves me not.
But all you will be left with is
a bunch of limp stems
and a boy who doesn't deserve
you if you have to question where
you stand.

- you can gift yourself flowers

Rain drops drip
like tears down his cheek.
you saw that he too was weak.

As a grin appeared on his face,
you learned his tears were
not from deficiency.

But rather all the joy
and life you breathe into him.

- tears don't always mean sadness

I saw his vision when
it was scribbled
on white boards
in the basement.

I believed in him
when everyone else
worried about his
radical risks to
follow his dreams.

I loved him whether we
were sipping
fine wine
or drinking
cheap beer.

I craved his ingenious
thoughts,
and endless affection.

*- it's easy to believe in someone
who believes just as much in you*

You are more than just
one voice in seven billion.
You are the world.
The world is in you.
Now is as good a time as ever
to speak up.

- it only takes one

Even on the cloudiest of days,
the sun is always there.
Though it's not in sight,
the true absence of it would be known.

- you are with me in spirit

The people telling you
all the things you are doing wrong,
or could be doing better
have their own set of problems
they are avoiding.
The life you live is not the life they live
and there is nothing wrong with that.

- no one is picture perfect

I know there can be a world
where schools aren't target practice,
night clubs don't turn into crime scenes,
landmarks aren't bombed.

I know there can be a world
where the color of your skin
doesn't determine whether you
may live or die
at the hands of those who
are supposed to protect all.

I know there can be a world
where my children
read about the devastations
in history books
but never experience them
repeating themselves.

- I know this world can be saved one day

You have to sip me like
whiskey,
not chug me like water.

- you will get drunk off my words

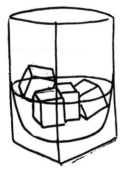

The last thing I want to do
is spend time whispering about a girl
who probably left the house today worrying
that how she looks would be talked about.

Six outfit changes,
only to put on the usual attire.
Hair curled into ringlets,
only to be defeated by fear of attention,
so she places a bun on top her head.

Her mind is hidden behind all the
physical traits you pick apart.
Her character can't be exposed if you
tear her down before she even opens
her mouth.

Think before you giggle about how she looks.
Maybe this was the first time she had
the courage to go out in a week.

- *xoxo I'm not a gossip girl*

My body is art.
Some see beauty
where other's see flaws.

- too bad I don't care about your critique

Even though your dreams seem
beyond the horizon,
you can reach them.
It may take as long as walking
20 miles in the desert,
or it may come as quick as
driving down the street.

- *ask, believe, receive*

Navigating her was like trying to
walk through the woods at midnight.
You risk the trek,
betting on
her voice to guide you safely
through the grounds.

- she is a force of nature

You can walk across a
stage and get handed a
diploma to reward you
for all the time you spent
researching,
studying,
writing,
stressing.

You can throw your
cap in the air and
cheers to an
unknown future.

You can go home,
apply for 9-to-5 jobs
to match your degree
and cross your fingers
for the phone call you need.

You can also skip
the college phase.
Live out of a tiny house,
sell your art online,
use coffee shop Wi-Fi.

- you can do what you want because it's
your own damn life

I have thighs that jiggle a little
when I run.
So what?
I like it that way.

Sometimes I eat ice cream
straight from the tub.
So what?
I like it that way.

I have small lines of growth
spread out across my hips.
So what?
I like it that way.

- *from a girl with body confidence*

People see luck
where hard work
really took place.
Dreams that took
a decade to create.

- nothing big just started yesterday

You are working hard
at a dream,
only to be pushed to the ground
time after time.
Remember, what you are doing
is world changing
and anything that big
needs a leader who can stay standing
in the biggest storms.

- fall seven times, get up eight

I want to die saying
I saw the world,
learned from the world,
tasted the world.
I don't need a six-figure salary
to experience the adventures.
I need an A-plus attitude
and a mind filled with belief.

- manifest your want into have

I Am More Than a Daydream

~

What makes you more than a daydream?

Share with me your
goals,
dreams,
and passions.
What do you love about yourself?
What brings you happiness?
Most importantly,
what are you are going to do to make
your dreams become your reality?

#IamMoreThanaDaydream

Acknowledgements

Thank you to all of those who purchased,
loved, and shared, my first two books
Bright Minds Empty Souls and
Uncaged Wallflower.
I am happy to have inspired so many
of you to live a more positive and
blissful life.
Every message, comment, or picture I see
of you all sharing my words warms my
heart.

To my love, my family, and my best
friends,
I am so grateful for your support and
encouraging words.

Also a very special thanks to all of my
writer friends for always helping and
supporting me!

To anyone who stumbles across this book,
I thank you.
Soak up every word, write in the margins,
highlight the lines you love, share your
thoughts and feelings of your favorite
poem with me.
Most importantly, learn from this book
that you are always more.

About The Author

JennaeCecelia.com

Instagram/Twitter: @JennaeCecelia

Jennae Cecelia is the self-published and best selling author of the poetry books, *Bright Minds Empty Souls* and *Uncaged Wallflower.*

She has developed a strong passion for writing uplifting poetry that encourages her readers to reach their full potential. *I Am More Than a Daydream* is the next book in the positive poetry series titled, JC Collection.

Made in the USA
Middletown, DE
16 March 2018